An Underwater Children's Christmas Musical

By Kari Lineberry

PART ONE: DIRECTOR'S NOTES

Have a great time being under the sea!
Kari Lineberry

MERRY FISH-MAS

An Underwater Children's Christmas Musical

Copyright © 2022 by Kari Lineberry

Photographs by Wayne Finehout

All rights reserved. No part of the book, (photos, music, or pint) may be reproduced or transmitted in any form or by any means, graphic, electronic, or mechanical, including photocopying, recording, audio or by any information storage retrieval system, without written permission of the publisher, KD Resources.

The purchase of this book gives permission to ONE BUYER to produce up to 15 paper copies of the script section (Part Two) of this book for their personal use only. Those copies may not be sold or duplicated in any way.

Published by KD Resources
Lewiston, Idaho
www.kdresources.org

Library of Congress ISBN

979-8-9853965-9-1

MERRY FISH-MAS

An Underwater Children's Christmas Musical

By Kari Lineberry

Play Description:

MERRY FISH-MAS! is a faith-based play that tells the Christmas story from an "underwater" perspective. Watch a variety of sea creatures sing, dance, and laugh while uniquely celebrating Christmas. This fun and whimsical musical includes the actor's script, (up to 15 copies), the Director's notes, web-based sound track and demo, and examples and directions for rehearsals, the set, props, and costumes that are fun and easy to make. This play is meant for inexperienced director's and includes speaking and non-speaking parts for up to 60 children. Parents will love watching their child perform in this play!

Set Design:

The idea is to set an atmosphere of being under the ocean. Use a lot of blue Christmas lights or spotlights.

You will need a shipwreck of some kind in the back ground. This can be made of carboard, painted on a hanging sheet or even as time consuming as cutting it from plywood and putting a back on it in order for it to stand up. Put blue and green Christmas lights around it so it is visible at all times. You can put a name on it called "The Bethlehem" or not. Either way works.

There needs to be a large shell for the turtle to come out of. You can use a large appliance box for this. Cut one side from the box. You should have three sides of the box left. Then 2 decorate the middle section to look like a shell. By folding the two other sides back use them to stand it up. Duct tape them to make a triangle shape if needed so it is free standing. Then put a stool or low, backless chair in front of it for the turtle to sit on. Cover the chair with a piece of blue or green cloth so it doesn't look like a chair. The turtle sits on it with back to the audience at the beginning of the play.

Stage Props:

Sea coral should be throughout the stage in different places. These can be easily assembled with cardboard boxes and bright colored pool noodles. Pinterest has some great ideas for this. Also you can cut a pool noodle circularly and wrap it around a microphone stand. This works great in the clown fish scene.

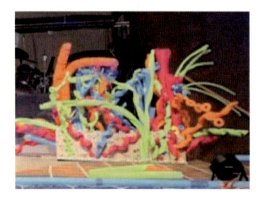

Other decorations in your facility could include making jelly fish to hang from the ceiling from paper lanterns and crepe paper or ribbon. Pinterest is always a good resource to learn how to do this.

Pictured are jelly fish hanging from the ceiling and a turtle ceiling decoration simulating that the audience is underwater.

Another fun idea to do at the front door as people walk in is to tack long pieces of a blue (light or dark) plastic tablecloth roll to the ceiling. Then cut out shapes of turtles from tag board and place it under the lights onto the plastic tablecloth. It gives the impression you are underwater with turtles swimming above you. You can purchase the plastic tablecloth in 100 feet rolls from several places. Commercial restaurant stores or at Orientaltrading.com. They are fairly inexpensive and go a long way.

Also, you should have some sea weed on your set if you have the room. An old Christmas tree can make a very good skeleton for a large piece of seaweed and coral. Tear 1 inch strips of cotton fabric. We got ours from a local thrift store for a few cents. If you know people who sew ask for left over fabric. You can use blues, purples, greens and even a dull red and brown. Then we placed coral made from pool noodles in the sea weed tree for the finishing touches.

Music:

Here are the directions to download the pre-recorded demos and sound tracks for Merry Fish-mas.

> *On any computer device*
>
> *Go to kdresources.org*
>
> *Click on "Book Store"*
>
> *Click on Merry Fish-mas Music*
>
> *Enter this code: KDRFishmas.*

This includes the sound track and a demo for each song.

For the prelude music and the music after the show use a classical piano or guitar Christmas CD with no vocal. Then play the audio only of a Youtube whale song video or sound affects CD of whale sounds. You will definitely have an "under the sea" sound. Play with it a little so that you get the sound you want.

Keep in mind that when you play Youtube videos you will have to deal with advertisements so you may want to or pre-record the whale songs from Youtube, or purchase whale sounds on an audio CD or mp3 file from a music app such as Amazon or iTunes.

Rehearsals:

This show can be done with one and a half hour rehearsals if the costumes and casting and choreography is done prior to rehearsals beginning.

Day 1 (Monday):

Divide the cast into four groups. Guppies and Jelly Fish, Clown Fish and Angel Fish, Snails and then have a one-on-one aid with the turtle. You will need an adult to teach and supervise each group. Each group will need a separate room or space so they are learning all at the same time.

Group 1-Guppies and Jelly fish will learn the opening song on this day. Have them do the song with the demo so they can learn the words and the dancing. Use the seaweed sticks to make the dancing easy and look very difficult even though it isn't. Use your creativity!

Group 2-Clown Fish and Angel Fish will learn their entire song and choreography on this day. Use the demo music to start with. Go through the words over and over since there is a lot to learn.

Group 3-Sea Snails will learn their entire song and choreography on this day. Spend extra time teaching them how to look and act like snails and remind them to be in slow motion at all times.

Group 4-Turtle and one-on-one aid will work on lines and music. If the turtle is not going to sing the School Song and/or Bethlehem's Ballad have the fish who will be singing one or both of those songs in this group too. Go over lines, choreography on this day for the School Song.

Day 2 (Tuesday):

Continue practicing in groups. Clown Fish and Angel Fish, Snails and then have a one-on-one aid with the turtle.

Group 1-Guppies and Jelly fish get this day off. They only need to come for Day 1,3, 6,8 and 9.

Group 2-Clown Fish and Angel Fish will continue to work on their song. Practice laughing loud.

Group 3-Sea Snails will continue learning to act like snails and to work on their song.

Group 4-Turtle and one-on-one aid will work on lines and music. Go over lines, choreography on this day for the School Song.

Day 3 (Wednesday):

Continue practicing in groups. Guppies, Clown Fish and Angel Fish, Snails and then have a one-on-one aid with the turtle.

Group 1-Guppies and Jelly fish continue working on their words and choreography.

Group 2-Clown Fish and Angel Fish will continue to work on their song.

Group 3-Sea Snails will continue learning to act like snails and to work on their song.

Group 4-Turtle and one-on-one aid will work on lines and music. Go over lines, choreography on this day for Bethlehem's Ballad.

Day 4 (Thursday):

Continue practicing in groups. Clown Fish and Angel Fish, Snails and then have a one-on-one aid with the turtle.

Group 1-Guppies and Jelly Fish get this day off. They only need to come for Day 1,3, 6,8 and 9.

Group 2-Clown Fish and Angel Fish will continue to work on their song. Practice laughing loud.

Group 3-Sea Snails will continue learning to act like snails and to work on their song.

Group 4-Turtle and one-on-one aid will work on lines and music. Go over lines, choreography on this day for Bethlehem's Ballad.

Day 5 (Friday):

Continue practicing in groups. Guppies, Clown Fish and Angel Fish, Snails and then have a one-on-one aid with the turtle.

Group 1-Guppies and Jelly Fish begin working on the words and choreography for the Finale'.

Group 2-Clown Fish and Angel Fish begin working on the words and choreography for the Finale'.

Group 3-Sea Snails will continue learning to act like snails and to begin working on the words and choreography for the Finale'.

Group 4-Turtle and one-on-one aid will work on lines and music. Go over lines, choreography on this day for the Finale'.

Day 6 (Monday):

All groups are together on this day. They will all be on the stage and learn the Finale'.

Day 7 (Tuesday):

All groups are together on this day. Start from the beginning and get clear through the play. It will be messy but keep going. Go through the blocking but don't spend too much time on special things. Get the main transitions down and assign the fish who will carry the "SAVIOR" sign and the starfish pole. If the turtle needs more work on lines see if he/she could have a little extra tutoring time with a one-on-one aid during non-rehearsal time.

Day 8 (Wednesday):

All groups are together on this day. Start from the beginning and get clear through the play again. Go through transitions again and be in the front row giving signals to help the actors remember where they go next.

Day 9 (Thursday):

Dress Rehearsal and cast party. Invite parents and family members to come on this night to be a very participatory audience. Coach them to be loud and engaged to encourage the actors. Have them all sit near the front but reserve the front row for the coaches and directors so they are in full view of the actors. Run through the play from start to finish and be sure to play the prelude and music following so the sound technician has a chance to do a run through also.

After the play have the kids put their costumes in their designated bags and make sure they have everything they need for the performance. Then have a cast party. Make dinner. Some great ideas are to have "oceany" type food so you are sticking with the "under the sea" theme. Pinterest has some great ideas.

Pictures are examples of crab sandwiches, octopus cream cheese spread, and ocean colored cupcakes.

Costumes:

Guppies-Pinterest has some elaborate fish costume ideas but the guppies can also be as simple as a face mask that the kids create themselves. Make sure they are lot of colors. These fish don't necessarily look like guppies. They are fish of all colors and sizes. Simplicity has a pattern for fish costumes, Orientaltrading.com has some and there are several other places online to get ideas too. Remember the more different kinds of fish costumes you can get the better. They should all be different if possible.

Turtle: Have the turtle dress in black or brown and wear a winter hat in brown or black too. Make a shell out of cardboard and attach a couple of straps so the actor can wear it like a backpack. There are several turtle costumes available online through the websites and apps already mentioned.

Angel Fish: This fish can really have any style of fish costume but make it white. You can take a pair of white mittens and sew some white tulle onto the bottom of them so there is a long wavy white flow to the hands when he/she swims around Mary and Joseph. It really adds a lot to the movement if you do this. Tulle can be purchased at any fabric store.

Clown Fish: These also can be any type of fish costume but they will need to be in the recognizable "Nemo" colors. They can be purchased or homemade masks.

Sea Snails: Make snail shells out of large pieces of cardboard. Attach a strap to the inside of each one so the actors can hold them in each hand. Have the actors dress in brown or black under their shells.

Jelly Fish: Use a clear umbrella with bubble wrap placed over the top. Clear strapping tape is best for attaching. Then cut strips of bubble wrap, crepe paper or both and attach them hanging down with the clear tape. The length of the strips will depend on the actor. Then have each actor hold a small flashlight in their hand with the umbrella handle. Point the flashlight straight up for a better affect. When the lights are dim this looks really "under the sea"!

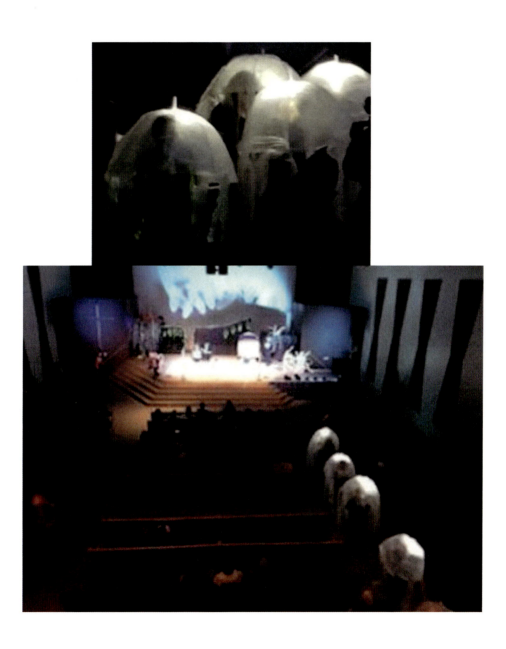

Show Notes:

MERRY FISH-MAS

While the pre-music is playing and before the lights come on the turtle takes his/her place on the shell. Lights come up and then from two separate entrances the guppies enter screaming and running in groups. The jelly fish enter behind them slowly gliding around the auditorium or across the stage (whichever is applicable) until they exit. Both groups of guppies come to a stop near center stage and the music begins.

We placed seaweed sticks on the floor of the stage prior to the show so that when the guppies made it to the stage they would each have one. The seaweed sticks were simply 18 inch dowel rods with a strip of blue fabric glued to them. The guppies used them for dancing.

Guppies Song:

We are the guppies from the reef, we swim all day but we never sleep

Oh, we love to be guppies.

Guppies, guppies, guppies…guppies, guppies, guppies

The drawback is when you're the dish, for eels and sharks and jelly fish

Oh, we love to be guppies Guppies, guppies, guppies…guppies, guppies, guppies

We swim and play, we swim and play all day (*repeat 4 times*)

Guppies, guppies, guppies…guppies, guppies, (*shout*) Guppies!

The spotlight slowly comes on center stage to expose a turtle. The turtle stands and yawns. The guppies gasp because they are startled for a moment and then start getting curious.

Guppie 1: What is an old turtle doing in a place like this? Aren't you afraid of the jelly fish?

Turtle: It's pretty hard for a silly jelly fish to sting through this shell and what's wrong with where I'm living? I've been here for many years and by now it seems kind of homey. (*The turtle takes his twig tree, puts a star fish on top and sets it up by or in his clam shell.*) It was here when I saw…them. (*Points to the ceiling*)

Guppie 2: Who's…?

Guppie 4: What's…?

All Guppies: …them?

Turtle: (*still pointing up*) They were right up there, right at the surface. It seems like it was just yesterday. The King of the land and sea had his two feet planted right there. I'd never seen it before and I've never seen it since. He walked on the water right above us. I couldn't believe my eyes! (*Guppies gasp*)

Guppie 3: But land lovers don't walk on water! They sink! I was almost killed by one once. He made such a big splash that it knocked me senseless. I just don't believe it! The next thing you'll say is his feet were "this" big! (*takes hands and motions them really wide mimicking a fish story*)

Turtle: Well that was only my first encounter with this land lover. He did more miracles than that. He was so wise that he told the fishermen that followed him that he would make them fishers of… MEN.

Guppie 1: What?! No more fishing for fish?

All Guppies: "Halleluia! We're saved!" (*jumping up and down and swimming all around*)

Guppie 3: Oh yeah! I am like a smart fish near a worm candy hook…I'm not swallowing it. You've got to come up with something better than that.

Turtle: Well, let me teach you a few things little fish, listen to an old, wise turtle…

(*Music begins.*)

If you have cast a person for the turtle part that doesn't have a great singing voice or the music is in the wrong key simply get someone else to sing the song and make your singer a guppy. If you choose to you can use the demo music with the voice already there to help your singer/singers.

School Song:

Turtle: (speaking) What do fish do best? They go to school, right? Gather around guppies!

(Turtle singing) Now it's time for history, To learn about a king,

From the Bible, God's own word

It's time for a Christmas story (*repeat*)

At this point you can actually have a large flannel board and use extra large Christmas story flannel graphs as the song is sung. Or you can make posters that show the characters of Christmas that the turtle holds up for the audience to see. Don't get too complicated. Just have the manger, the shepherds, the wisemen for this part of the play.

Long ago in Bible times, exciting things took place

God sent His son through a virgin birth

Jesus saved the whole human race (*repeat*)

(Pause singing for dancing section)

He was born in Bethlehem, Shepherds came to see

Wisemen came to bring him gifts

That is the Christmas story (*repeat*)

Just so you learn this really good, We'll do it so you understand,

We'll tell the story from the deep

Under the sea and not on dry land *(repeat) (repeat full verse)*

Turtle: (speaking) C'mon fishes. It's time for the Christmas story!

Mary and Joseph enter holding a small fish stuffed animal as the baby Jesus.

(Music begins)

If you don't have enough kids for extra parts, just use guppies here. They can double as the Mary and Joseph fish.

Turtle: Long ago in a faraway sea, a fish named Mary was chosen to have a tiny smolt salmon. This little fishy was very special.

Lots of things can go on during this song since the music is slow and seems a bit boring all by itself.

Bethlehem's Ballad:

Have the angel swim around Mary during the first two lines and then swim around Joseph for the next two lines.

1. **An angel came to Mary and said she would have a son**

    And to call him Jesus, He would be the One.

    And Joseph dreamed that his job was to take care of the boy

    Knowing that his God through him would bring such joy

During the chorus have the turtle hold up a globe and spin it and point to land and sea each time it is sung. At the same time have some of the guppies roll a beach ball back and forth. Have some of the fish do the wave or the backstroke dance.

Chorus:
And as he grew he became King of land of sea
And as he grew he became King of land of sea

A great idea for the baby Jesus: Take a stuffed animal fish and hand sew or safety pin it to the back of a cheap glove or mitten the same color as the Mary fish costume. Have the person playing Mary put the glove on and make movements with her hand to make it look like the fish is swimming. When verse two starts have the Mary fish pull the glove out from behind a stage prop and quickly slip it on her hand.

2. So Mary had the baby, Jesus was this baby's name

His earthly keeper, Joseph knew he was to be a King

Jesus was so special and they knew he came from God

They would take good care of him like any parent should

Have a pool noodle cut out like a sling shot or something like it to seem like a toy. During the verse the Joseph fish pulls it out and it playing with the baby fish.

Again, during the chorus have the turtle hold up a globe and spin it and point to land and sea each time it is sung. At the same time have some of the guppies roll a beach ball back and forth. Have some of the fish do the wave or the backstroke dance.

Chorus:

And as he grew he became King of land of sea

And as he grew he became King of land of sea

Have a couple of the guppies hold up a large sign attached on both sides to a dowel rod that simply reads "SAVIOR" in big, bright, bold lettering. They can move the rods so the sign looks like it is floating in the water.

Bridge:

He's the Savior of the world

He's the Savior of the world

He's the Savior of the world

He's the Savior of the world

Again, during the chorus have the turtle hold up a globe and spin it and point to land and sea each time it is sung. At the same time have some of the guppies roll a beach ball back and forth. Have some of the fish do the wave or the backstroke dance.

Chorus:

And as he grew he became King of land of sea

And as he grew he became King of land of sea

Clown fish enter from the side or back of the room laughing loudly and swimming around.

If you have extra kids to cast have more than two clown fish. The extras can just be laughers and singers. It's sure to make for a more hilarious scene.

Turtle: (*pointing to the clown fish*) There were clown fish… I mean shepherds… in the open water taking care of…well…what they take care of… when a stranger came to them.

(*Two clown fish take their places in front of the microphone stands as if they are stand up comedians.*)

Angel Fish: (*enters from back stage*) Behold, I bring you good tides of great joy!

Clown: Good tides of great joy? We'll show you good tides of great joy…Hey Bozo…why is a tropical fish always in trouble?

Bozo: I don't know, why is a tropical fish always in trouble?

Clown: Because he's always swimming in hot water! Get it? (*elbows the Angel Fish*) Hot water?

(*All clown fish roll in laughter*)

Angel Fish: That wasn't exactly what I had in mind.

Bozo: Oh, I've got one!

Angel Fish: Great. (*being sarcastic*)

Bozo: What did the boy octopus say to the girl octopus?

Clown: I don't know, what did the boy octopus say to the girl octopus?

Bozo: I wanna hold your hand hand hand hand hand hand hand hand

(*All clown fish roll in laughter once again*)

Clown: One more! One more! Why did the whale cross the road?

Bozo: I don't know. Why did the whale cross the road?

Clown: To get to the other tide!!! Ha! Ha! Ha!

(*All laugh again*)

Angel: Please, I didn't need a comedy show. I have good news clowns! A baby is born.

Bozo: But that's not funny at all. Angel: It may not be funny but it's important. This baby is the King of all land and sea. He came to save the world from their sins.

Clown: Oh, that's a big deal.

Angel: Yeah! (*sarcastic*) You'll find the baby wrapped in kelp and laying in the hull of a shipwreck of called the Bethlehem. (*Behind her breath*) Okay, so for you land lovers out there it was in swaddling clothes and lying in a manger. You get the picture.

Clown: Is the baby funny? I mean does he have a sense of humor?

Bozo: (*Music begins.*) Yeah, is he full of great jokes and does he make funny faces?

Bop Shoo Bottom Bop Song:

1. **The ocean's really classy with it's clams, coral, and pearls, But it's the funny fish that makes it**
   beautiful, it's the clown fish of the world

2. **So the Angel fish is lovely with her scales so snowy white She brings us good news of a baby who**

   is born for us tonight

Have the clowns use sunglasses for the first line of verse 3. They can hang them on or under their costumes for easy accessibility.

3. **We're sure that baby's cool now, He's the savior of the sea But does he know some jokes or**

   does he play ping pong He must cuz He makes us free.

   (wipeout percussion section)

4. **Let's go find the baby, Jesus in the Bethlehem And worship Him cuz he's the savior of all sea**

   and land

5. **(bridge) Bop shoo bottom, bottom Bop shoo bottom fish**
   Bop shoo bottom, bottom Bop shoo bottom fish

   Bop shoo bottom, bottom Bop shoo bottom fish

   Bop shoo bottom, bottom, bottom fish

(*wipeout percussion section*)

3. We're sure that baby's cool now, He's the savior of the sea

    But does he know some jokes or does he play ping pong

    He must cuz He makes us free.

4. Let's go find the baby, Jesus in the Bethlehem

5. And worship Him cuz he's the savior of all sea and land

Angel: Yeah, sure, all of that. Work with me here clowns, you should probably go see if you can find him don't you think?

(*Some jelly fish enter from one side and the fish all swim away from it and then wind up back at center stage again. At the same time: lights go dim except to spotlight the snails as they enter doing a synchronized walk moving their heads up and down slowly like a snail would.*)

Turtle: And after the clown fish heard of the baby King three wise sea snails from the Eastern current made their way across fathoms of seas to find him. (*Music begins.*) They carried gifts for the baby.

Have each sea snail take a name to sing solo to. The first one is Es, the second is Car and the third is Go. Each can solo their names and sing the rest of the song together. If you don't have strong vocalists play the demo and have the kids sing along with it.

Es, Car, Go Song:

We are Es, Car, and Go

We are Es, Car, and Go

We are three wise sea snails from the Eastern current

We traveled far across the gooey sea floor.

We bring pearls, sea cucumbers and sand dollars

To worship the baby king, we should've brought more

Have one or two guppies carry a star glued to the top of a dowel rod and run back and forth across the stage which each time the words "star" and "fish" are sung. Have the choreography coincide with each time the star goes by. Example: the guppy runs to one side while the line "We followed the star fish" and the snail turn heads as the guppy runs by and turn their shells sharply on the word "fish". Then do it again for the next time they sing it. With big awkward shells this is very funny.

We followed the star…fish

We followed the star…fish

Es, Car, Go (*repeat*)

(*Snail dance section*)

We followed the star…fish

We followed the star…fish

We are Es, Car, Go

They are Es, Car, Go

Es, Car, Go

They followed the star fish

Es, Car, Go

They are Es, Car, Go

Es, Car, Go

(When the song is finished the sea snails come center stage to the ship wreck. All the fish gather round for the underwater manger scene.)

Turtle: This baby was born to save all land and sea just the way that God had planned and so each one that accepts this little King can have an eternal home in heaven with Him forever. I remember the power he had as He got older. The awe that I felt in my heart at the very sight of Him… He is the King of the world. Joy to the whole world, a Savior is born to take away the sins of the world! (*Music begins*.)

You can have the clown fish front and center when you sing the "Joy to the World…Joy to the ocean" parts. The guppies do the "Here comes Jesus, here comes Jesus" section. Have the sea snails do the "Have yourself a merry little fishmas" sections. If you don't' have a lot of good vocalists have everyone sing the whole thing and just divide up the dance parts. Remember to feel free to use the demo recording also.

Finale'

Joy to the world…Joy to the ocean

Joy to the world…Joy to the ocean

Here comes Jesus, Here comes Jesus right from Bethlehem

He has come to show His love in the heart of every man.

O Come all ye faithful, joyful and triumphant…

Joy to the world…Joy to the ocean

Joy to the world…Joy to the ocean

Have yourself a merry little Fish-mas,

Let the Yule tide flow-oh-oh-oh.

Have yourself a merry little Fish-mas,

So the world will know-oh-oh-oh!

Joy to the world…Joy to the ocean

Joy to the world…Joy to the ocean

Joy! (*echo*) Joy! (*echo*) Joy! (*echo*) Joy! (*echo*)

While the clown fish are singing "Joy to the world" in this section, the guppies are picking up shells for the next part. Have them bang some real shells together during the "Jingle Shells" part. It just adds some awesome percussion to the song.

Jingle shells, jingle shells, jingle all the way!

Oh what fun it is to ride in a clam pulled by a ray! Hey!

Jingle shells, jingle shells, jingle all the way!

Jesus came to save the world. He was born on Christmas day!

Have yourself a merry little Fish-mas,

Let the Yule tide flow-oh-oh-oh.

Have yourself a merry little Fish-mas,

So the world will know-oh-oh-oh!

Joy to the world…Joy to the ocean

Joy to the world…Joy to the ocean

Joy! (echo) Joy! (echo) Joy! (echo) Joy! (echo) Joy!

(shout) JOY!

On the last "JOY!" have the clown fish pop some confetti poppers. You can get them reasonably priced at Orientaltrading.com. Order enough to have them practice with them first so they can actually pop them on que.

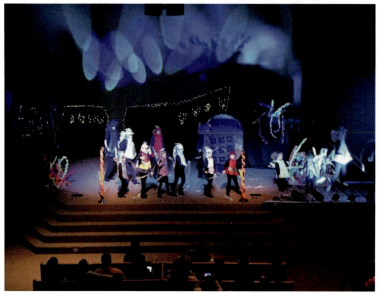

Do a curtain call once the play is over.

THE END

An Underwater Children's Christmas Musical

By Kari Lineberry

PART TWO: SCRIPT

MERRY FISH-MAS

An Underwater Children's Christmas Musical

Copyright © 2022 by Kari Lineberry

Photographs by Wayne Finehout

All rights reserved. No part of the book, (photos, music, or pint) may be reproduced or transmitted in any form or by any means, graphic, electronic, or mechanical, including photocopying, recording, audio or by any information storage retrieval system, without written permission of the publisher, KD Resources.

The purchase of this book gives permission to ONE BUYER to produce up to 15 paper copies of the script section (Part Two) of this book for their personal use only. Those copies may not be sold or duplicated in any way.

Published by KD Resources
Lewiston, Idaho
www.kdresources.org

Library of Congress ISBN

979-8-9853965-9-1

MERRY FISH-MAS

An Underwater Children's Christmas Musical

By Kari Lineberry

Scene 1: Lights are dim.

From two separate entrances the guppies enter screaming and running in groups. Lights come up gradually. The jelly fish enter behind them slowly gliding around the auditorium or across the stage (whichever is applicable) until they exit. Both groups of guppies come to a stop near center stage.

(*Music begins.*)

Guppies Song:

We are the guppies from the reef, we swim all day but we never sleep

Oh, we love to be guppies.

Guppies, guppies, guppies...guppies, guppies, guppies

The drawback is when you're the dish, for eels and sharks and jelly fish

Oh, we love to be guppies

Guppies, guppies, guppies…guppies, guppies, guppies

We swim and play, we swim and play all day (repeat 4 times)

Guppies, guppies, guppies…guppies, guppies, (shout) Guppies!

The spot light slowly comes on center stage to expose a turtle. The turtle stands and yawns. The guppies gasp because they are startled for a moment and then start getting curious.

Guppie 1: What is an old turtle doing in a place like this? Aren't you afraid of the jelly fish?

Turtle: It's pretty hard for a silly jelly fish to sting through this shell and what's wrong with where I'm living? I've been here for many years and by now it seems kind of homey. (*The turtle takes his twig tree, puts a star fish on top and sets it up by or in his clam shell.*) It was here when I saw…them. (*Points to the ceiling*)

Guppie 2: Who's…?

Guppie 4: What's…?

All Guppies: …them?

Turtle: (*still pointing up*) They were right up there, right at the surface. It seems like it was just yesterday. The King of the land and sea had his two feet planted right there. I'd never seen it before and I've never seen it since. He walked on the water right above us. I couldn't believe my eyes! (*Guppies gasp*)

Guppie 3: But land lovers don't walk on water! They sink! I was almost killed by one once. He made such a big splash that it knocked me senseless. I just don't believe it! The next thing you'll say is his feet were "this" big! (*takes hands and motions them really wide mimicking a fish story*)

Turtle: Well that was only my first encounter with this land lover. He did more miracles than that. He was so wise that he told the fishermen that followed him that he would make them fishers of… MEN.

Guppie 1: What?! No more fishing for fish?

All Guppies: "Halleluia! We're saved!" (*jumping up and down and swimming all around*)

Guppie 3: Oh yeah! I am like a smart fish near a worm candy hook…I'm not swallowing it. You've got to come up with something better than that.

Turtle: Well, let me teach you a few things little fish, listen to an old, wise turtle…

(*Music begins.*)

School Song:

Turtle: (*speaking*) What do fish do best? They go to school, right? Gather around guppies!

(*Turtle singing*) **Now it's time for history, To learn about a king,**

From the Bible, God's own word

It's time for a Christmas story (repeat)

Long ago in Bible times, exciting things took place

God sent His son through a virgin birth

Jesus saved the whole human race (*repeat*)

(Pause singing for dancing section)

He was born in Bethlehem, Shepherds came to see

Wisemen came to bring him gifts

That is the Christmas story (*repeat*)

Just so you learn this really good, We'll do it so you understand,

We'll tell the story from the deep

Under the sea and not on dry land (*repeat*) (*repeat full verse*)

Turtle: (*speaking*) C'mon fishes. It's time for the Christmas story!

Mary and Joseph enter holding a small fish stuffed animal as the baby Jesus.

(*Music begins*)

Turtle: Long ago in a far away sea, a fish named Mary was chosen to have a tiny smolt salmon. This little fishy was very special.

Bethlehem's Ballad:

An angel came to Mary and said she would have a son

And to call him Jesus, He would be the One.

And Joseph dreamed that his job was to take care of the boy

Knowing that his God through him would bring such joy

Chorus:

And as he grew he became King of land of sea

And as he grew he became King of land of sea

So Mary had the baby, Jesus was this baby's name

His earthly keeper, Joseph knew he was to be a King

Jesus was so special and they knew he came from God

They would take good care of him like any parent should

Chorus:

And as he grew he became King of land of sea

And as he grew he became King of land of sea

Bridge:

He's the Savior of the world

He's the Savior of the world

He's the Savior of the world

He's the Savior of the world

Chorus:

And as he grew he became King of land of sea

And as he grew he became King of land of sea

Clown fish enter from the side or back of the room laughing loudly and swimming around.

Turtle: (*pointing to the clown fish*) There were clown fish… I mean shepherds… in the open water taking care of…well…what they take care of… when a stranger came to them.

Clown fish take their places in front of the microphone stands.

Angel Fish: (*enters from back stage*) Behold, I bring you good tides of great joy!

Clown: Good tides of great joy? We'll show you good tides of great joy…Hey Bozo…why is a tropical fish always in trouble?

Bozo: I don't know, why is a tropical fish always in trouble?

Clown: Because he's always swimming in hot water! Get it? (*elbows the Angel Fish*) Hot water?

(*All clown fish roll in laughter*)

Angel Fish: That wasn't exactly what I had in mind.
Bozo: Oh, I've got one!

Angel Fish: Great. (*being sarcastic*)

Bozo: What did the boy octopus say to the girl octopus?

Clown: I don't know, what did the boy octopus say to the girl octopus?

Bozo: I wanna hold your hand hand hand hand hand hand hand hand

(*All clown fish roll in laughter once again*)

Clown: One more! One more! Why did the whale cross the road?

Bozo: I don't know. Why did the whale cross the road?

Clown: To get to the other tide!!! Ha! Ha! Ha!

(*All laugh again*)

Angel: Please, I didn't need a comedy show. I have good news clowns! A baby is born.

Bozo: But that's not funny at all.

Angel: It may not be funny but it's important. This baby is the King of all land and sea. He came to save the world from their sins.

Clown: Oh, that's a big deal.

Angel: Yeah! (*sarcastic*) You'll find the baby wrapped in kelp and laying in the hull of a shipwreck of called the Bethlehem. (*Behind her breath*) Okay, so for you land lovers out there it was in swaddling clothes and lying in a manger. You get the picture.

Clown: Is the baby funny? I mean does he have a sense of humor?

(*Music begins.*)

Bozo: Yeah, is he full of great jokes and does he make funny faces?

Bop Shoo Bottom Bop Song:
1. **The ocean's really classy with it's clams, coral, and pearls, But it's the funny fish that makes it beautiful, it's the clown fish of the world**
2. **So, the Angel fish is lovely with her scales so snowy white She brings us good news of a baby who is born for us tonight**
3. **We're sure that baby's cool now, He's the savior of the sea But does he know some jokes or does he play ping pong He must cuz He makes us free. (wipeout percussion section)**
4. **Let's go find the baby, Jesus in the Bethlehem And worship Him cuz he's the savior of all sea and land**
5. *(bridge)* **Bop shoo bottom, bottom Bop shoo bottom fish**

Bop shoo bottom, bottom Bop shoo bottom fish

Bop shoo bottom, bottom Bop shoo bottom fish

Bop shoo bottom, bottom, bottom fish

(*wipeout percussion section*)

3. We're sure that baby's cool now, He's the savior of the sea But does he know some jokes or does he play ping pong He must cuz He makes us free.

4. Let's go find the baby, Jesus in the Bethlehem

And worship Him cuz he's the savior of all sea and land

Angel: Yeah, sure, all of that. Work with me here clowns, you should probably go see if you can find him don't you think?

(*Some jelly fish enter from one side and the fish all swim away from it and then wind up back at center stage again. At the same time: lights go dim except to spotlight the snails as they enter doing a synchronized walk moving their heads up and down slowly like a snail would.*)

Turtle: And after the clown fish heard of the baby King three wise sea snails from the Eastern current made their way across fathoms of seas to find him. *(Music begins.)* They carried gifts for the baby.

Es, Car, Go Song:

We are Es, Car, and Go

We are Es, Car, and Go

We are three wise sea snails from the Eastern current

We traveled far across the gooey sea floor.

We bring pearls, sea cucumbers and sand dollars

To worship the baby king, we should've brought more

We followed the star…fish We followed the star…fish

Es, Car, Go *(repeat)*

(Snail dance section)

We followed the star…fish

We followed the star…fish

We are Es, Car, Go

They are Es, Car, Go

Es, Car, Go

They followed the star…fish

Es, Car, Go

They are Es, Car, Go

Es, Car, Go

(When the song is finished the sea snails come center stage to the ship wreck. All the fish gather round for the underwater manger scene.)

Turtle: This baby was born to save all land and sea just the way that God had planned and so each one that accepts this little King can have an eternal home in heaven with Him forever. I remember the power he had as He got older. The awe that I felt in my heart at the very sight of Him… He is the King of the world. Joy to the whole world, a Savior is born to take away the sins of the world!

(Music begins.)

Finale'

Joy to the world…Joy to the ocean

Joy to the world…Joy to the ocean

Here comes Jesus, Here comes Jesus right from Bethlehem

He has come to show His love in the heart of every man.

O Come all ye faithful, joyful and triumphant…

Joy to the world…Joy to the ocean

Joy to the world…Joy to the ocean

Have yourself a merry little Fish-mas,

Let the Yule tide flow-oh-oh-oh.

Have yourself a merry little Fish-mas,

So the world will know-oh-oh-oh!

Joy to the world…Joy to the ocean

Joy to the world…Joy to the ocean

Joy! (*echo*) Joy! (*echo*) Joy! (*echo*) Joy! (*echo*)

Jingle shells, jingle shells, jingle all the way!

Oh, what fun it is to ride in a clam pulled by a ray! Hey!

Jingle shells, jingle shells, jingle all the way!

Jesus came to save the world. He was born on Christmas day!

Have yourself a merry little Fish-mas,

Let the Yule tide flow-oh-oh-oh.

Have yourself a merry little Fish-mas,

So the world will know-oh-oh-oh!

Joy to the world…Joy to the ocean

Joy to the world…Joy to the ocean

Joy! (*echo*) **Joy!** (*echo*) **Joy!** (*echo*) **Joy!** (*echo*) **Joy!** (*shout*) **JOY!**

THE END

Made in the USA
Las Vegas, NV
12 September 2022